Reconstruction

Researching American History

edited by
JoAnne Weisman Deitch

*After the Civil War, schools were available in most areas of the South for Black children. This sketch was made in Charleston, S.C. at the Zion School. (*Harper's Weekly, *December 1866)*

Discovery Enterprises, Ltd.
Carlisle, Massachusetts

All rights reserved. No part of this book may be reproduced, stored in a retrieval system, or transmitted in any form or by any means, electronic, mechanical, photocopied, recorded, or otherwise, without prior written permission of the authors or publisher, except for brief quotes and illustrations used for review purposes.

First Edition © Discovery Enterprises, Ltd., Carlisle, MA 2001

ISBN 978-1-57960-072-3

Library of Congress Catalog Card Number 2001090237

Printed in the United States of America

Subject Reference Guide:

Title: *Reconstruction*
Series: *Researching American History*
edited by JoAnne Weisman Deitch

Post-Civil War Reconstruction - U. S. History

Credits:

Cover illustration: *African-American Voting in Richmond*, William L. Sheppard, artist, *Frank Leslie's Illustrated Newspaper,* November 18, 1871, p. 152.

Other illustrations are credited where they appear in the book

Contents

About the Series 4
   Reading the Historical Documents 4

Introduction 5
   Lincoln seeks to bind up the nation's wounds 6
   A Southerner recalls the end of the war 7
   A Northerner's point of view 8

The South after the War 9
   Economic disaster 13

Plans for Reconstruction 16
   Lincoln's Ten Percent Plan 16
   Andrew Johnson Carries on with Reconstruction Plans 19

The Freedmen's Bureau 21
   Mary Ames' Diary 23
   Radical Republicans Spoke Out 24
   Thaddeus Stevens' Speech 24
   Harper's Weekly kept the people informed 26
   Blacks spoke out, as well 29
   "Reconstruction" by Frederick Douglass 29

The Joint Committee on Reconstruction 31
   Testimony of Homer A. Cook 31
   Testimony of the Rev. James W. Hunnicutt 32
   Testimony of James D. B. DeBow 33
   Booker T. Washington 35

The Civil Rights Bill 36
   Harper's Weekly editorial 36

The Reconstruction Act 38
   Congressional Reconstruction Policy 38
   A Southerner's point of view 39
   The Ku Klux Klan 41
   Testimony taken at a Senate Hearing on terrorist activity 41
   Blacks in Office 43
   Senator Davis of Kentucky 44
   Senator James Nye of Nevada replies to Davis of Kentucky 44

Carpetbaggers and Scalawags by Cheryl Edwards 45
   Horace Greeley Campaigns 45
   Albert Griffin, a Republican from Georgia, defends the carpetbaggers .. 46
   Song about Carpetbaggers 46

President Johnson's Impeachment Trial 48
   Harper's Weekly editorial on the Civil Rights Bill 36

The Black Vote by Cheryl Edwards 50

Research Activities/Things to Do 52

Suggested Further Reading 56

About the Series

Researching American History is a series of books which introduces various topics and periods in our nation's history through the study of primary source documents.

Reading the Historical Documents

On the following pages you'll find words written by people during or soon after the time of the events. This is firsthand information about what life was like back then. Illustrations are also created to record history. These historical documents are called **primary source materials**.

At first, some things written in earlier times may seem difficult to understand. Language changes over the years, and the objects and activities described might be unfamiliar. Also, spellings were sometimes different. Below is a model which describes how we help with these challenges.

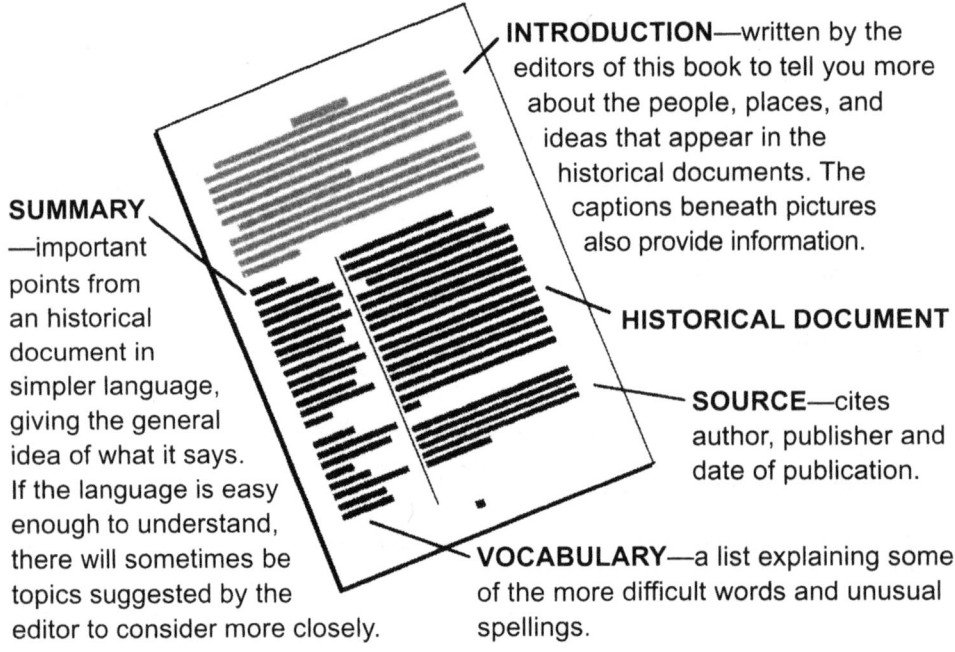

INTRODUCTION—written by the editors of this book to tell you more about the people, places, and ideas that appear in the historical documents. The captions beneath pictures also provide information.

SUMMARY—important points from an historical document in simpler language, giving the general idea of what it says. If the language is easy enough to understand, there will sometimes be topics suggested by the editor to consider more closely.

HISTORICAL DOCUMENT

SOURCE—cites author, publisher and date of publication.

VOCABULARY—a list explaining some of the more difficult words and unusual spellings.

In these historical documents, you may see three periods (…) called an ellipsis. It means that the editor has left out some words or sentences. You may see some words in brackets, such as [and]. These are words the editor has added to make the meaning clearer. When you use a document in a paper you're writing, you should include any ellipses and brackets it contains, just as you see them here. Be sure to give complete information about the author, title, and publisher of anything that was written by someone other than you.

Introduction

When the Civil War ended in April of 1865, President Lincoln was hopeful that the "Reconstruction" of the divided South and North would commence, healing and restoring the nation's wounds. However, only five weeks after his second inauguration, Lincoln was assasinated, leaving the war-torn nation in despair and facing as many conflicts as had been experienced during the war itself.

The subsequent reconstruction of the nation was left to a new president, Andrew Johnson, and the "Radical Republicans" who took charge of Congress. Although many congressmen wanted the South to rejoin the Union wholeheartedly, working together to repair the wounds inflicted on the country by the war, many others resisted the South's speedy reentry into the government.

Between 1865 and 1870, the Thirteenth, Fourteenth, and Fifteenth Amendments to the U. S. Constitution were passed, making slavery illegal in the country, giving freed slaves the full rights of citizenship, and giving freed Black men the right to vote.

The South, still struggling with long-held feelings of hatred and prejudice, resisted. The North was not able to erase the sentiments of generations of slave-owners and all of the emotional baggage that came with it, so that true reconstruction of the country lasted well into the 20th century, and still influences civil rights issues, even today.

The War had brought an end to slavery and a promise to restore the Union, but it left many complicated issues to resolve. The South's economy had been destroyed, and its people were hungry and homeless. Political bickering divided the country and turned the Reconstruction process into another battleground.

As historian Joel Williamson noted in his book, *After Slavery*:

Freedom was a nominal legacy of the war, yet telling the slave that he was free did not make him so. Ultimately, the Negro had to establish his freedom by some deliberate, conscious act entirely his own, or he would remain a slave in fact, if not in name. Emancipation simply gave him that choice.... By whatever means the Negro learned of emancipation, the most obvious method of affirming his freedom was simply to desert the site of his slavery and the presence of his master....

Vocabulary:
emancipation = The act of being freed
legacy = something handed down or bequeathed
nominal = in name only

Source: Joel Williamson, *After Slavery: The Negro in South Carolina During Reconstruction, 1861-1877*. Univ. of North Carolina Press, 1975, pp. 32-3.

Lincoln seeks to bind up the nation's wounds

Lincoln had made his plan of action clear in his second inaugural speech.

Summary:
With no bad feelings, and with a charitable spirit, let's try to repair the divided nation, help those who were in the battle and the widows and orphans, so we can have lasting peace.

Vocabulary:
malice = ill will

..."With malice toward none, with charity for all, with firmness in the right as God gives us to see the right, let us strive on to finish the work we are in, to bind up the nation's wounds, to care for him who shall have borne the battle and for his widow and orphan, to do all which may achieve and cherish a just and lasting peace among ourselves and with all nations."

Helping the South's homeless and hungry was the government's most urgent problem. The South's infrastructure had been totally destroyed. Cities had been burned to the ground, and railways, roads, and bridges were impassable.

Consider this:
With so many soldiers killed or injured, who was available to "reconstruct" the South?

Burned-out printing mill in Richmond, Virginia is representative of the destruction in Southern cities after the war. April, 1865. (Library of Congress)

There were severe shortages of raw materials and manpower which hindered rebuilding efforts. Poverty and suffering touched all social classes. Wealthy aristocratic plantation owners lost everything, and most were little better off than the freed slaves who had once worked their fields. The freed slaves, who had been emancipated in 1863, were among the most destitute of the population. They were illiterate, homeless, and without any immediate hope for better opportunities. The Civil War had totally paralyzed the South.

A Southerner recalls the end of the war

The last act of the tragedy had closed... The Civil War ended, — the bloodiest, most destructive war the world ever saw. The earth had been baptized in the blood of five hundred thousand heroic soldiers, and a new map of the world had been made.

The ragged troops were straggling home... along the country roads. There were no mails, telegraph lines or railroads. The men were telling the story of the surrender. White-faced women dressed in coarse homespun met them at their doors and with quivering lips heard the news.

Surrender!

A new word in the vocabulary of the South — a word so terrible in its meaning that the date of its birth was to be the landmark of time. Henceforth all events would be reckoned from this; "before the Surrender," or "after the Surrender."

Desolation everywhere marked the end of an era. Not a cow, a sheep, a horse, a fowl, or a sign of animal life save here and there a stray dog, to be seen. Grim chimneys marked the site of once fair homes. Hedgerows of tangled blackberry briar and bushes showed where a fence had stood before war breathed upon the land with its breath of fire and harrowed it with teeth of steel.

These tramping soldiers looked worn and dispirited. Their shoulders stooped, they were dirty and hungry. They looked worse than they felt, and they felt that the end of the world had come.

Summary:
Summarize this document in your own words.

Vocabulary:
Desolation = ruin; a wasteland
harrow = break up and level the land

Source: Thomas Dixon, Jr., *The Leopard's Spots—A Romance Of The White Man's Burden—1865-1900*. New York: Doubleday, Page & Co., 1902, p. 4.

Summary:
The bitterness of the war would have passed, but the process of reconstruction in the ruined cities and towns of the South was extremely painful. Lincoln's plans and the distinguished work of previous lawmakers, gave way to wild and unruly behavior.

Vocabulary:
conciliatory = soothing; meant to win over
fanaticism = extreme zeal or dedication to a religious or political cause

A Northerner's point of view

"The bitterness of the war would soon have passed away, but the horror of reconstruction sank deeper into the soul of the South than even the memory of devastated lands and of cities laid in ashes. It is painful now to dwell upon the folly and fanaticism which made that period the darkest in all American history. The wise and conciliatory plans of Lincoln were forgotten by the Northern Radicals. Legislative halls which had been honored by the presence of learned jurists and distinguished law-givers, were filled with a rabble of plantation hands, who yelled and jabbered like so many apes...."

Source: H. T. Peck, LL.D., Columbia College, from *Documenting the American South,* found on http://docsouth.unc.edu/thomas/thomas.html

Civil War artist, Gilbert Gaul, painted this scene entitled "Return Home," portraying a Confederate soldier who has just found his home in ruins after the war.

The South after the War

Frances Butler Leigh described her travels through the South, the year after the war was over.

Consider this:
Why does the author think that southerners could only see ruin ahead?

The year after the war between the North and South, I went to the South with my father to look after our property in Georgia and see what could be done with it.

The whole country had of course undergone a complete revolution. The changes that a four years' war must bring about in any country would alone have been enough to give a different aspect to everything; but at the South, besides the changes brought about by the war, our slaves had been freed; the white population was conquered, ruined, and disheartened, unable for the moment to see anything but ruin before as well as behind, too wedded to the fancied prosperity of the old system to believe in any possible success under the new. And even had the people desired to begin at once to rebuild their fortunes, it would have been in most cases impossible, for in many families the young men had perished in the war, and the old men, if not too old for the labour and effort it required to set the machinery of peace going again, were beggared, and had not even money enough to buy food for themselves and their families, let alone their negroes, to whom they now had to pay wages as well as feed them.

On March 22, 1866, my father and myself left the North. The Southern railroads were many of them destroyed for miles, not having been rebuilt since the war, and it was very questionable how we were to get as far as Savannah, a matter we did accomplish however, in a week's

(continued on next page)

Things to do:

Compare the expression of feelings of the soldier in the painting on page 8 with those expressed in this journal entry. Which is more effective? Why do you think so?

Have you ever tried to express your feelings in writing? In art?

Vocabulary

listless = lacking energy or enthusiasm

time... [We reached] Richmond at four o'clock on Sunday morning....

. . . .

I can hardly give a true idea of how crushed and sad the people are. You hear no bitterness towards the North; they are too sad to be bitter; their grief is overwhelming. Nothing can make any difference to them now; the women live in the past, and the men only in the daily present, trying, in a listless sort of way, to repair their ruined fortunes. They are like so many foreigners, whose only interest in the country is their own individual business. Politics are never mentioned, and they know and care less about what is going on in Washington than in London.

. . . .

The fine houses have fallen to decay or been burnt down; the grounds neglected and grown over with weeds; the plantations left, with a few exceptions, to the negroes; olive groves choked up with undergrowth; stately date-palms ruthlessly burnt down by negroes to make room for a small patch of corn, where there were hundreds of acres, untilled, close at hand; a few solitary men eking out an existence by growing fruit trees and cabbages, by planting small patches of cotton or corn, by hunting deer, or by selling whiskey to the negroes.

Source: Frances Butler Leigh, *Ten Years on a Georgia Plantation After the War.* London: R. Bentley and Son, 1883. From *THE SOUTH: A Documentary History,* by Ina Woestemeycr Van Noppen, Princeton, New Jersey: D. Van Nostrand Company, Inc., 1958.

Both white southerners and freed slaves endured tremendous suffering after the war. The following passages describe problems faced by both races.

...The general destitution has rendered many kindly disposed people unable to do anything for the negroes who were formerly their slaves, and who might be supposed to have some claims upon them for temporary assistance on that account, and there is much suffering among the aged and infirm, the sick and helpless, of this class of people.... It is a common, and everyday sight in Randolph County, that of women and children, most of whom were formerly in good circumstances, begging for bread from door to door. Meat of any kind has been a stranger to many of their mouths for months. The drought cut off what little crops they hoped to save, and they must have immediate help or perish....

By far the greatest suffering exists among the whites. Their scanty supplies have been exhausted, and now they look to the government alone for support. Some are without homes of any description. This seems strange and almost unaccountable. Yet on one road leading to Talladega I visited four families, within fifteen minutes' ride of the town, who were living in the woods, with no shelter but pine boughs, and this in mid-winter. Captain Dean, who accompanied me, assured me that upon the other roads leading into town were other families similarly situated. These people have no homes. They were widows, with large families of small children. Other families, as provisions fail, will wander in for supplies, and I am fearful the result will be a camp of widows and orphans. If possible, it should be prevented; and yet I saw about thirty persons for whom shelter must be provided, or death will speedily follow their present exposure and suffering.

(continued on next page)

Summary:
The poverty that everyone is experiencing is making it impossible for the southern whites to help their former slaves. The old and the sick are suffering, and women and children, who used to be fine, are begging for food.

They have no farm animals to provide meat, and the lack of rain has ruined the crops. They must have help or they will die.

The worst suffering is that of the white people. Many have no homes, and are forced to live in the woods. Many are women and children, and, if they don't get help soon, they will die from exposure to the weather.

Summary:
Summarize this excerpt in your own words.

Vocabulary:
contraband = illegal or smuggled goods; in the Civil War this term referred to escaped slaves who were taken behind Union lines

impunity = without punishment or harm

Source: First excerpt, quoted from the Senate Executive Document No. 27, Congress, I Session. Second excerpt, quoted from the Senate Executive Document No. 2, 39 Congress, I Session.

When the war came to a close, the labor system of the South was already much disturbed. During the progress of military operations large numbers of slaves had left their masters and followed the columns of our armies; others had taken refuge in our camps; many thousands had enlisted in the service of the national government. Extensive settlements of negroes has been formed along the seaboard and the banks of the Mississippi, under the supervision of army officers and treasury agents, and the government was feeding the colored refugees, who could not be advantageously employed, in the contraband camps. Many slaves had been removed by their masters, as our armies penetrated the country, either to Texas or to the interior of George and Alabama. Thus a considerable portion of the laboring force had been withdrawn from its former employments. But a majority of the slaves remained on the plantations to which they belonged, especially in those parts of the country which were not touched by the war, and where, consequently, the emancipation proclamation was not enforced by the military power. When...the report went...out that their liberation was...a fixed fact, large numbers of colored people left the plantations; many flocked to our military posts and camps to obtain the certainty of their freedom, and others walked away merely for the purpose of leaving the place on which they had been held in slavery, and because they could now go with impunity. Still others, and their number was by no means inconsiderable, remained with their former masters and continued their work on the field.... The country found itself thrown into that confusion which is naturally inseparable from a change so great and so sudden....

Economic Disaster

Historian Walter Lynwood Fleming described the South in desperate economic conditions in the following selections.

From Harper's Ferry to New Market, which is about eighty miles...the country was almost a desert. ...We had no cattle, hogs, sheep, or horse or anything else. The fences were all gone. Some of the orchards were very much injured, but the fruit trees had not been destroyed. The barns were all burned; chimneys standing without houses, and houses standing without roof, or door, or window.

Much land was thrown on the market at low prices—three to five dollars an acre for land worth fifty dollars. The poorer lands could not be sold at all, and thousands of farms were deserted by their owners. Everywhere recovery from this agricultural depression was slow....

. . . .

There were few stocks of merchandise in the South when the war ended, and Northern creditors had lost so heavily through the failure of Southern merchants that they were cautious about extending credit again. Long before 1865 all coin had been sent out in contraband trade through the blockade. That there was a great need of supplies from the outside world is shown by the following statement of General Boynton:

Window-glass has given way to thin boards, in railway coaches and in the cities. Furniture is marred and broken, and none has been replaced for four years. Dishes are cemented in various styles, and half the pitchers have tin handles. A complete set of crockery is never seen, and in very few families is there enough to set a table....

(continued on next page)

Consider this:

In a poor economy, such as that found in the southern states after the war, some people were able to profit from the losses of others. At what other time in U. S. history has that been the case? Describe your findings.

Consider this:
The account given here describes a host of problems facing the people of the South. List them in the order of importance, with the biggest problem first, and the rest following.

Can you imagine how you would have handled a similar situation if you had lived during this time?

A set of forks with whole tines is a curiosity. Clocks and watches have nearly all stopped. ...Hair brushes and tooth brushes have all worn out; combs are broken. ...Pins, needles, and thread, and a thousand such articles, which seem indispensable to housekeeping, are very scarce. Even in weaving on the looms, corncobs have been substituted for spindles. Few have pocket knives. In fact, everything that has heretofore been an article of sale at the South is wanting now. At the tables of those who were once esteemed luxurious providers you will find neither tea, coffee, sugar, nor spices of any kind. Even candles, in some cases, have been replaced by a cup of grease in which a piece of cloth is plunged for a wick.

This poverty was prolonged and rendered more acute by the lack of transportation. Horses, mules, wagons, and carriages were scarce, the country roads were nearly impassable, and bridges were in bad repair or had been burned or washed away. Steamboats had almost disappeared from the rivers. Those which had escaped capture as blockade runners had been subsequently destroyed or were worn out. Postal facilities, which had been poor enough during the last year of the Confederacy, were entirely lacking for several months after the surrender.

. . . .

The South faced the work of reconstruction not only with a shortage of material and greatly hampered in the employment even of that but still more with a shortage of men....

...The poorer whites who had lost all were close to starvation. In the white counties which had sent so large a proportion of men to the army the destitution was most acute. In many families the breadwinner had been killed in war.

After 1862, relief systems had been organized in nearly all the Confederate States for the purpose of aiding the poor whites, but these organizations were disbanded in 1865....

. . . .

Acute distress continued until 1867; after that year there was no further danger of starvation. Some of the poor whites, especially in the remote districts, never again reached a comfortable standard of living; some were demoralized by too much assistance; others were discouraged and left the South for the West or the North. But the mass of the people accepted the discipline of poverty and made the best of their situation.

The difficulties, however, that beset even the courageous and the competent were enormous. The general paralysis of industry, the breaking up of society, and poverty on all sides bore especially hard on those who had not previously been manual laborers. Physicians could get practice enough but no fees; lawyers who had supported the Confederacy found it difficult to get back into the reorganized courts because of the test oaths and the competition of "loyal" attorneys; and for the teachers there were few schools. We read of officers high in the Confederate service selling to Federal soldiers the pies and cakes cooked by their wives, of others selling fish and oysters which they themselves had caught, and of men and women hitching themselves to plows when they had no horse or mule.

Source: Walter Lynwood Fleming, *The Sequel of Appomattox: A Chronicle of the Reunion of the States.* New Haven: Yale University Press, 1919.

Consider this:
What does the author mean when he says "Some were demoralized by too much assistance"?

What are the "disciplines of poverty" to which he refers?

Plans for Reconstruction

The period in America's history which is referred to as the Reconstruction period is considered to be the years 1865, following the end of the Civil War, to 1877 (although many of its facets carried over well into the 20th century.) There were several major issues concerning those who worked at reconstructing the nation, which had been torn apart during the war.

First, who was responsible for the secession of the Confederates, and should they be punished? Second, what would the states which had joined the Confederacy have to do to once again be accepted as part of the Union? Third, how would the newly-won freedom of thousands of slaves be protected? And, last, how could the South survive without its economic system of slave labor?

Years of struggle and debate followed within the Federal government. Agencies were put in place to oversee the education, voting rights, and job opportunities for the former slaves.

The Republican Party dominated national politics, as most of the southern Democrats in Congress had left during the war years. Radical Republicans, such as senators Benjamin Wade of Ohio and Charles Sumner of Massachusetts, and Representatives, Thaddeus Stevens and George W. Julian, of Pennsylvania and Indiana, took the lead in the fight to rebuild the South—and the nation.

Even while the war was still being fought, Republicans worked on plans for the eventual reuniting of the southern states. In the Wade-Davis bill, Radical Republicans would require 50 percent of a state's white males to swear loyalty to the U. S. Constitution, before being allowed to rejoin the Union. President Lincoln's Ten Percent Plan called for only 10% of white males to take an oath of allegiance to the Union. (He vetoed the Wade-Davis bill in 1864.) On December 8, 1863, the President presented his plan, excerpted below.

Summary:
I grant a full pardon to each person who participated in the rebellion, and restore their rights and property (except for slaves) on the condition that they take the following oath:

Lincoln's Ten Percent Plan

...I, Abraham Lincoln, President of the United States, do proclaim, declare, and make known to all persons who have, directly or by implication, participated in the existing rebellion, except as hereinafter excepted, that a full pardon is hereby granted to them and each of them, with restoration of all rights of property, except as to slaves and in property cases where rights of third persons have intervened, and upon the condition that every such person shall take and subscribe an oath and thenceforward keep and maintain said oath inviolate, and which oath shall be registered for permanent preservation and shall be of the tenor and effect following, to wit:

I,_____ _____, do solemnly swear, in presence of Almighty God, that I will henceforth faithfully support, protect, and defend the Constitution of the United States and the Union of the States thereunder; and that I will in like manner abide by and faithfully support all acts of Congress passed during the existing rebellion with reference to slaves, so long and so far as not repealed, modified, or held void by Congress or by decision of the Supreme Court; and that I will in like manner abide by and faithfully support all proclamations of the President made during the existing rebellion having reference to slaves, so long and so far as not modified or declared void by decision of the Supreme Court. So help me God.

The persons excepted from the benefits of the foregoing provisions are all who are or shall have been civil or diplomatic officers or agents of the so-called Confederate Government; all who have left judicial stations under the United States to aid in the rebellion; all who are or shall have been military or naval officers of the so-called Confederate Government above the rank of colonel in the army or of lieutenant in the navy; all who left seats in the United States Congress to aid the rebellion; all who resigned commissions in the Army or Navy of the United States and afterwards aided the rebellion; and

(continued on next page)

Summary:
The oath:
I swear to support the Constitution of the United States and the Union, all acts of Congress, and proclamations of the President and decisions of the Supreme Court.

This applies to everyone except those who were agents or military officers (above a specified rank) of the Confederacy, or those who left seats held in Congress to join the rebels; or those who treated Blacks unlawfully.

Vocabulary:
inviolate = intact; not violated
tenor = the exact meaning of the words of a document, not their effect

Summary:

I further proclaim that in the 11 states which seceded, not less than 1/10th of the people who voted in the 1860 election shall re-establish a state government for their state. The Congress (not the President) will determine if newly-elected representatives from those states will be admitted to serve.

all who have engaged in any way in treating colored persons, or white persons in charge of such, otherwise than lawfully as prisoners of war, and which persons may have been found in the United States service as soldiers, seamen, or in any other capacity.

And I do further proclaim, declare, and make known that whenever, in any of the States of Arkansas, Texas, Louisiana, Mississippi, Tennessee, Alabama, Georgia, Florida, South Carolina, and North Carolina, a number of persons, not less than one-tenth in number of the votes cast in such State at the Presidential election of the year A.D. 1860, each having taken the oath aforesaid, and not having since violated it, and being a qualified voter by the election law of the State existing immediately before the so-called act of secession, and excluding all others, shall reestablish a State government which shall be republican .... such shall be recognized as the true government of the State....

. . . .

... It may be proper to say...that whether members sent to Congress from any State shall be admitted to seats constitutionally rests exclusively with the respective Houses, and not to any extent with the Executive....

Given under my hand at the city of Washington, the 8th day of December, A.D.,1863....

Source: *A Compilation of the Messages and Papers of the Presidents, 1789-1902,* by James D. Richardson, Washington, published by authority of Congress, 1902, Vol. VI.

Andrew Johnson Carries on with Reconstruction Plans

When Andrew Johnson, a Democrat from Tennessee, assumed the Presidency upon Lincoln's assassination in April 1865, he took on the enormous responsibility of reconstructing the Union. His first annual message as president, given on December 4, 1865, suggested that he would follow much of what Lincoln had planned.

...I have...gradually and quietly, and by almost imperceptible steps, sought to restore the rightful energy of the General Government and of the States. To that end provisional governors have been appointed for the States' conventions called, governors elected, legislatures assembled, and Senators and Representatives chosen to the Congress of the United States....

The next step which I have taken to restore the constitutional relations of the States has been an invitation to them to participate in the high office of amending the Constitution.... The evidence of sincerity in the future maintenance of the Union shall be put beyond any doubt by the ratification of the proposed amendment to the Constitution, which provides for the abolition of slavery forever within the limits of our country.....

. . . .

Good faith requires the security of the freedmen in their liberty and their property, their right to labor, and their right to claim the just return for their labor.... The country is in need of labor, and the freedmen are in need of employment, culture, and protection.... Let us encourage them to honorable and useful industry, where it may be beneficial to themselves and to the country....

Summary:
Summarize this speech in your own words.

Vocabulary:
imperceptible = not capable of being perceived (seen or understood)

But shortly, it became apparent that Johnson held a much more lenient position toward former members of the Confederacy, and he offered amnesty to all who pledged allegiance to the Constitution, except for a few of the wealthiest plantation owners, who had to apply personally for a pardon.

He appointed a governor for each state, who was to call a convention for the purpose of creating a new state constitution, which made slavery illegal, and which would bring the state quickly back into the Union. Southern whites were delighted by the leniency of the new president, and conformed to Johnson's plans. They immediately began to create laws which restricted the rights of the newly-freed slaves. Although these laws varied from state to state, the Black Codes, as they were called, all intended to limit the rights of former slaves, and all angered those in the North working toward reconstructing the Union.

When Congress reconvened in December of 1865, the Republican majority refused to accept the new representatives from the Southern states, chosen under Johnson's plan, and long and bitter debates began over Reconstruction.

In 1866, Johnson vetoed two bills which had strong Republican support, the continuation of the Freedmen's Bureau and the Civil Rights Bill. Both were enacted, despite the President's veto.

Consider this:
This *Harper's Weekly* cartoon by Thomas Nast portrays Johnson kicking out the Freedmen's Bureau with his veto. Scattered Black people are coming out and falling down. Do you think that political cartoons can have as strong a message as the written word?

Find several contemporary cartoons in a magazine or newspaper, and bring them in to share with the class.

The Freedmen's Bureau

The federal government created the Freedmen's Bureau to administer emergency assistance to former slaves and white southerners after the war. The Bureau's volunteers set up schools, fed the hungry, found temporary housing for the homeless, and helped the freed slaves adjust to their new lives. Journalist John T. Trowbridge from Massachusetts wrote about his observations of a school run by the Freedmen's Bureau. An excerpt from his work follows.

There were three thousand pupils in the freedmen's schools. The teachers for these were furnished, here as elsewhere, chiefly by benevolent societies in the North. Such of the citizens as did not oppose the education of the blacks, were generally silent about it. Nobody said of it, "That is freedom! That is what the Yankees are doing for them.!"

Visiting these schools in nearly all the Southern States, I did not hear of the white people taking any interest in them. With the exception of here and there a man or woman inspired by Northern principles, I never saw or heard of a Southern citizen, male or female, entering one of those humble school-rooms....

The wonder with me was, how these "best friends" could be so utterly careless of the intellectual and moral interests of the freedmen. For my own part, I could never enter one of those schools without emotion. They were often held in old buildings and sheds good for little else. There was not a school room in Tennessee furnished with appropriate seats and desks. I found a similar condition of things in all the States. The pews of colored churches, or plain benches in the vestries, or old chairs with boards laid across them in some loft over a shop, or out-of-

(continued on next page)

Summarize:
Summarize this passage in your own words.

Vocabulary:
benevolent = charitable, well-wishing, humane

Vocabulary:

taint = spoiling influence

doors on the grass in summer, — such was the usual scene of the freedmen's schools.

...I never visited one of any size in which there were not two or three or half a dozen children so nearly white that no one would have suspected the negro taint. From these, the complexion ranges through all the indescribable mixed hues, to the shining iron black of a few pure-blooded Africans, perhaps not more in number than the seemingly pure-blooded whites. The younger the generation, the lighter the average skin; by which curious fact one perceives how fast the race was bleaching under the "peculiar" system or slavery.

Source: J.T. Trowbridge, *A Picture of the Desolated States and the Work of Restoration*. Hartford, Conn., 1868.

Teacher Harriet Murray, with students, Elsie and Puss, February 1866. (Penn Community Services)

Mary Ames' Diary

As a young woman from Boston, Mary Ames volunteered to become a teacher. In 1865, she went to South Carolina to teach former slaves how to read and write.

The school was in a building once used as a billiard room, which accommodated a large number of pupils. We often had a hundred and twenty, and when word went forth that supplies had come, the number increased. Indeed, it was so crowded that we told the men and women they must stay away to leave space for the children, as we considered teaching them more important.

When we made out the school report..., we were surprised that out of the hundred, only three children knew their age, nor had they the slightest idea of it; one large boy told me he was "Three months old." The next day many of them brought pieces of wood or bits of paper with straight marks made on them to show how many years they had lived. One boy brought a family record written in a small book.

...In January smallpox broke out among the soldiers quartered on our place. Many of our scholars took it, and we closed the school for five weeks. We escaped, although in continual danger, for the negroes, even when repulsively sick, were so eager for our gifts of clothing that they forced their way to our very bedrooms, and our carryall, drawn by men, was used to carry the patients to the improvised hospital.... When on Monday, February [26th], we began school again, we had thirteen pupils. One of them, when asked if there was smallpox at her plantation, answered, "No, the last one died Saturday." On the third day one hundred children had come back.

Source: Mary Ames, *A New England Woman's Diary in Dixie in 1865*. Springfield, 1906.

Things to do:
Imagine that you are a teacher from New England who has volunteered to teach recently-freed slaves in the South. Write a journal entry about the school you're working at, describing the students, the school building, etc. Base your journal on other documents that you have found on the internet or in the library.

Consider this:
It is very evident upon their emancipation that former slaves were eager to learn to read and write. Most had been deprived of a formal education while in slavery. Why had the southern slave-owners been so opposed to their slaves being educated?

Radical Republicans Spoke Out

Opposition to President Johnson's lenient Reconstruction Plan sprung up in Congress. A group of Radical Republicans put forth their own version of a plan. The two leaders of the Radical Republicans were Congressman Thaddeus Stevens of Pennsylvania and Senator Charles Sumner of Massachusetts. They proposed a harsh set of polices that the Southern States had to fulfill in order for them to rejoin the Union. In 1865, Thaddeus Stevens made a speech in Lancaster, Pennsylvania, where he promoted the idea of confiscating property in the South and redistributing it among freed slaves. The following is an excerpt from his speech.

Summary:
We think the government ought to punish the rebels, to make them so weak that they will never again endanger the Union. We should reform their state governments, and seize their property to repay the national debt, which they caused by their rebellion.

Vocabulary:
belligerents = hostile people
condign = deserved; adequate
defacto = actual
forfeitures = things that have been surrendered
instigated = urged on; stirred up
republicans = people who favor a democratic or constitutional form of government

Thaddeus Stevens' Speech

...We hold it to be the duty of the Government to inflict condign punishment on the rebel belligerents, and so weaken their hands that they can never again endanger the Union; and so reform their municipal institutions as to make them republican in spirit as well as in name.

We especially insist that the property of the chief rebels should be seized and appropriated to the payment of the National debt, caused by the unjust and wicked war which they instigated.

How can such punishments be inflicted and such forfeitures produced without doing violence to established principles.

Two positions have been suggested.

1st—To treat those States as never having been out of the Union.

2nd—To accept the position in which they placed themselves as severed from the Union; an independent government defacto, and an enemy alien to be dealt with according to the laws of war....

In reconstruction...no reform can be effected in the Southern States if they have never left the Union. But reformation must be effected; the foundation of their institutions, both political, municipal and social must be broken up and relaid, or all our blood and treasure have been spent in vain. This can only be done by treating and holding them as a conquered people. Then all things which we can desire to do, follow with logical and legitimate authority. As conquered territory Congress would have full power to legislate for them.... They would be held in a territorial condition until they are fit to form State Constitutions, republican in fact not in form only, and ask admission into the Union as new States....

We propose to confiscate all the estate of every rebel belligerent whose estate was worth $10,000, or whose land exceeded two hundred acres in quantity. Policy if not justice would require that the poor, the ignorant, and the coerced should be forgiven. They followed the example of their wealthy and intelligent neighbors. The rebellion would never have originated with them. Fortunately those who would thus escape form a large majority of the people, though possessing but a small portion of the wealth. The proportion of those exempt compared with the punished would be I believe about nine tenths.

Source: Richard Nelson Current, *Old Thad Stevens*. Madison: University of Wisconsin Press, 1942.

Summary:
The two positions are: To treat the states as if they had never left the Union, or, to treat them as enemies of our country.

We must treat them as conquered people. We should oversee their formation of new state governments before they may ask for admission to the Union as new states.

We propose to confiscate the property of the wealthy people who participated in the rebellion. The poor, uneducated people should be forgiven, because they can't be held responsible for what they did. I believe that about 1/10th of the people would be affected by this plan.

Vocabulary:
coerced = forced
confiscate = seized by an authority

Harper's Weekly *kept the people informed*

One of the most important publications to keep the average citizen informed was *Harper's Weekly*. Two editorials and an illustration follow.

Summary:
There are a few points about Reconstruction that have not been discussed in detail. Although four million slaves have been freed, there remains a great deal of prejudice in the South. There are some politicians among Southern Whites, who would like to regain power. To prevent this, we must give Blacks the right to vote.

Some think that the Blacks would be manipulated by politicians on both sides, but they would have their own ideas, their own leaders. Because they were oppressed for so long, and because they were involved in the war as Union soldiers, they would probably vote for democratic policies.

Vocabulary:
unscrupulously = acting without moral integrity; having no scruples

...There are points in the policy of reconstruction that have hitherto been little discussed, but which must very soon assume important phases. The emancipation of four millions of slaves, it is thought, will but partially effect the work of political regeneration in the South. If the reports which reach us have any truth, it is certain that there is a large class in the South whose prejudice against the sentiments held at the North is as strong as ever before. There are men and women there who will teach their children to hate the name of Northern men. There are politicians of this class who will strive again for power, which they will wield as unscrupulously as they have ever done. A barrier against the possibility of such an exercise of power must be set the very first, or we shall have no tranquil peace for many years. The only remedy is to not to simply free but also to enfranchise the negroes.

Give the negroes a vote and they will most certainly be courted by both parties at the South. It may be objected that they will thus become merely the tools of politicians. But it must be remembered that freedom will excite new activities in these black men. They will have leaders of their own; they will have sentiments of their own; and the policy which they will most naturally adopt will be that which will bring them into alliance with the poor loyal whites of the South. Besides, their memories of the past oppression of which they have been the victims, their memory of the part which colored soldiers have played in the war for the Union—all these will bind them to a purely Democratic policy.

Source: *Harper's Weekly*, May 13, 1865, page 1

This illustration by A. R. Waud, entitled "The First Vote," appeared on the front cover of Harper's Weekly, *November 16, 1867.*

Summary:

Lincoln was a strong president because he was patient. In this regard, he differs from Johnson, who likes to fight. When he became president after Lincoln's assassination, Johnson said he was resolved to support the Constitution and the Union, but he only really supports those who agree with his opinions.

It seems that now, those who supported the Union during the war disagree with many of his ideas, and those who rebelled against the Union seem to agree with and support Johnson.

Vocabulary:

despotic = having the absolute power of a despot
imprudently = unwisely
predecessor = one who came before someone in office
vehemently = forcefully; passionately

The Political Situation

Mr. Lincoln was strong because he was patient. His patience enabled him to know and to weigh exactly the force of opinions. If he had constantly said upon the vital points of the war, "My mind is made up. I am not to be moved," he would have lacked precisely the distinctive quality of his greatness as a man and of his fitness as President.

President Johnson's temperament differs from President Lincoln's as General Jackson's did from General Washington's. Mr. Johnson likes a fight. All his life he has been a sturdy political champion. He has been trained in the most orthodox discipline of the most despotic of parties, and he gives blows as well as takes them. At the close of a fierce war he stepped into the Presidency over the body of his predecessor murdered by those who would gladly have killed him; and his grim resolution to maintain the Constitution and Union, as he understood them, promised to be inflexible against all whose views differed from his own. But forgetting, as it seems to us, that the most patriotic men may honestly differ in a crisis like the present, he rather imprudently recognizes as the only friends of the Union those who support his policy in every point, without weighing the probable and obvious motives of such support in many quarters. Thus while he declares himself with peculiar emphasis the defender of the Union and Constitution it is remarkable that those who have not shown during the war that they were its enemies doubt the wisdom of some of his measures, while those who have been the open and bloody or secret and treacherous foes of the Union, now vehemently applaud every word he utters and every act he does....

Source: *Harper's Weekly,* April 14, 1866, p. 226.

Blacks spoke out, as well

Frederick Douglass

"Reconstruction"
by Frederick Douglass

We, the undersigned members of a Convention of colored citizens of the State of Virginia, would respectfully represent that, although we have been held as slaves, and denied all recognition as a constituent of your nationality for almost the entire period of the duration of your Government, and that by *your permission* we have been denied either home or country, and deprived of the dearest rights of human nature: yet when you and our immediate oppressors met in deadly conflict upon the field of battle— the one to destroy and the other to save your Government and nationality, *we*, with scarce an exception, in our inmost souls espoused your cause, and watched, and prayed, and waited, and labored for your success.

When the contest waxed long, and the result hung doubtfully, you appealed to us for help, and how well we answered is written in the rosters of the two hundred thousand colored troops now enrolled in your service; and as to our undying devotion to your cause, let the uniform acclamation of escaped prisoners, *"whenever we saw a black face we felt sure of a friend,"* answer.

(continued on next page)

Summary:
Summarize Douglass' speech in your own words.

Vocabulary:
constituent = a component; part of the whole
espoused = gave full support to
oppressors = those who persecute by force
subjugated = conquered or subdued
waxed long = became longer

Consider this:

What does Douglass mean by the phrase "lip deep"?

What does he believe is the only important right for Blacks to have, now that they've been freed?

Vocabulary:

malignity = intense ill will
subjugated = overcome, defeated

Well, the war is over, the rebellion is "put down," and we are *declared* free! Four fifths of our enemies are paroled or amnestied, and the other fifth are being pardoned, and the President has, in his efforts at the reconstruction of the civil government of the States, late in rebellion, left us entirely at the mercy of these subjugated but unconverted rebels, in *everything* save the privilege of bringing us, our wives and little ones, to the auction block.... We *know* these men—know them *well*—and we assure you that, with the majority of them, loyalty is only "lip deep," and that their professions of loyalty are used as a cover to the cherished design of getting restored to their former relations with the Federal Government, and then, by all sorts of "unfriendly legislation," to render the freedom you have given us more intolerable than the slavery they intended for us.

We warn you in time that our only safety is in keeping them under Governors of the *military persuasion* until you have so amended the Federal Constitution that it will prohibit the States from making any distinction between citizens on account of race or color. In one word, the only salvation for us besides the power of the Government, is in the *possession of the ballot*. Give us this, and we will protect ourselves....

Trusting that you will not be deaf to the appeal herein made, nor unmindful of the warnings which the malignity of the rebels are constantly giving you, and that you will rise to the height of being just for the sake of justice, we remain yours for our flag, our country and humanity.

Source: *"Reconstruction"* by Frederick Douglass, *The Atlantic Monthly,* December 1866. An address to the Loyal Citizens and Congress of the United States of America adopted by a convention of Negroes held in Alexandria, Virginia, from August 2 to 5, 1865.

The Joint Committee on Reconstruction

At the opening of the thirty-ninth Congress in 1865, the Radical Republicans were looking for a way to promote their agenda. They wanted to weaken and destroy President Johnson's Reconstruction plans. To dramatize their point, they chose not to let the new Southern Congressmen take their seats. They then formed a Joint Congressional Committee made up of six Senators and nine Representatives. This Committee was asked to study the Reconstruction issues, and then determine if the ex-Confederate States were entitled to be represented in Congress. The Radical Republicans believed that Congress should make Reconstruction policy, not the President.

The following testimonies were taken from the Joint Committee on Reconstruction.

Testimony of Homer A. Cook

Q. What effect has President Johnson's liberal policy in granting pardons and amnesties to rebels had upon the minds of the secessionists there; has it made them more or less favorable to the government of the United States?

A. I can, perhaps, better answer that question by saying that every unconditional Union man of my acquaintance in that state is opposed to that policy.

Q. How do the secessionists feel about it?

A. They claim the President as their friend in that matter.

. . . .

Q. How do they speak of the majority in the two houses of Congress?

A. In terms of deep and malignant hatred.

Q. What are some of the epithets they apply to them, if they apply any?

A. They are spoken of as radicals, who would ruin their country if they cannot rule it....

(continued on next page)

Things to do:
Find out who Homer A. Cook was.

Vocabulary:
epithets = a term used to characterize a person or thing

Rev. James W. Hunnicutt was one of the most radical southerners of the era.

Consider this:

Many Southerners thought that the government should repay them for their slaves, when they were freed. What do you think? Defend your answer.

Consider the discussions going on now (in 2001) about our government making reparations to all blacks whose ancestors were brought to this country as slaves. How would you determine who has a direct line of ancestry, and who would be expected to pay?

Vocabulary:
allay = lessen or relieve
copperhead party = Northerners who sympathized with the South during the Civil War
repudiate = to reject or refuse to recognize

Testimony of the Rev. James W. Hunnicutt

Q. What is the effect of President Johnson's policy of reconstruction there?

A. ...They are all in favor of President Johnson's policy of reconstruction. As soon as they get their ends served by him they would not touch him, but he is their man now. They say that in 1868 the South will be a unit, and that with the help of the copperhead party of the North they will elect a President. They do not care to have slavery back, but they will try and make the federal government pay them for their slaves. A man from Virginia told me today that they would be paid for their Negroes. This gentleman lost forty Negroes. This is their idea; they do not want slavery back, but they want to be paid for their slaves. They say that unless you accept their debt they will repudiate yours. They say they are not interested in this government....

Q. They propose to get back into the Union for the purpose of restoring the Constitution?

A. Yes, sir, and the testimony of the Negroes will not be worth a snap of your finger, and all this is done for policy. A Negro can come and give his testimony, and it passes for what it is worth with the courts. They can do what they please with it; there are judges, the lawyers, and the jury against the Negro, and perhaps every one of them is sniggering and laughing while the Negro is giving his testimony.

Q. Has not the liberal policy of President Johnson in granting pardons and amnesties rather tended to soothe and allay their feelings towards the government of the United States?

A. No, sir, not towards the government of the United States nor towards the Union men.

James D. B. DeBow, a southern writer and editor, gave testimony to the Joint Committee on Reconstruction on the treatment of African Americans in southern cities.

Testimony of James D. B. DeBow

Q. What is your opinion of the necessity or utility of the Freedmen's Bureau, or of any agency of that kind?

A. I think if the whole regulation of the Negroes, or freedmen, were left to the people of the communities in which they live, it will be administered for the best interest of the Negroes as well as of the white men. I think there is a kindly feeling on the part of the planters towards the freedmen. They are not held at all responsible for anything that has happened. They are looked upon as the innocent cause. In talking with a number of planters, I remember some of them telling me they were succeeding very well with their freedmen, having got a preacher to preach to them and a teacher to teach them, believing it was for the interest of the planter to make the Negro feel reconciled; for, to lose his services as a laborer for even a few months would be very disastrous....Leave the people to themselves, and they will manage very well. The Freedmen's Bureau, or any agency to interfere between the freedman and his former master, is only productive of mischief....

Q. What do you find the disposition of the people as to the extension of civil rights to the blacks—the right to sue and enforce their contracts and to hold property, real and personal, like white people?

A. I think there is a willingness to give them every right except the right of suffrage....

(continued on next page)

Vocabulary:
reconciled = resolved; settled

TO THE Freedmen.

WENDELL PHILLIPS ON LEARNING TO READ AND WRITE.

BOSTON, July 16, 1865.

My Dear Friend:

You ask me what the North thinks about letting the Negro vote. My answer is, *two-thirds* of the North are willing he should vote, and *one* of these *thirds* is determined he *shall* vote, and will not rest till he does. But the opposition is very strong, and I fear we may see it put off for many a year.

Possibly there may be an agreement made, that those who can read and write shall vote, and no others.

Urge, therefore, every colored man *at once* to learn to read and write. His right to vote may very likely depend on that. Let him lose no time, but learn to read and write *at once*.

Yours truly,

Mr. JAMES REDPATH.   WENDELL PHILLIPS.

A public letter by Abolitionist Wendall Phillips warned that literacy might be a condition of black suffrage. (Library of Congress)

Vocabulary:
emissaries = agents, sent to advance the interests of others

Q. Suppose the Negroes were to vote now, what would be the influences operating upon them as to the exercise of that vote?

A. The Negro would be apt to vote with his employer if he was treated well. That is his character. They generally go with their employer; but it is probable they would be tampered with a great deal. There would be emissaries sent among them to turn their minds; so that, although I understand some prominent men think the Negro would generally vote with his master, I doubt it....

Source: Hans L. Trefousse, *Background For Radical Reconstruction.* Boston: Little Brown and Co., 1970. Excerpts taken from the Hearings of the Joint Committee on Reconstruction, the Select Committee on the Memphis Riots and Massacres, and the Select Committee on the New Orleans Riots - 1866 and 1867.

Booker T. Washington

Booker T. Washington, an educator and spokesman for African Americans, believed that a vocational education was the best route to economic independence for Blacks. In his book, *Up from Slavery: An Autobiography,* he talked about Reconstruction. He later founded the Tuskeegee Institute in Alabama.

...It could not have been expected that a people who had spent generations in slavery, and before that generations in the darkest heathenism, could at first form any proper conception of what an education meant. In every part of the South, during the Reconstruction period, schools, both day and night, were filled to overflowing with people of all ages and conditions, some being as far along in age as sixty and seventy years. The ambition to secure an education was most praiseworthy and encouraging. The idea, however, was too prevalent that, as soon as one secured a little education, in some unexplainable way he would be free from most of the hardships of the world...

. . . .

During the whole of the Reconstruction period our people throughout the South looked to the Federal Government for everything, very much as a child looks to its mother. This was not unnatural. The central government gave them freedom, and the whole Nation had been enriched for more than two centuries by the labour of the Negro. Even as a youth, and later in manhood, I had the feeling that it was cruelly wrong in the central government, at the beginning of our freedom, to fail to make some provision for the general education of our people in addition to what the states might do, so that the people would be better prepared for the duties of citizenship.

Things to do:

Summarize Washington's thoughts on the education of Blacks.

Where, in his opinion, did the post-Civil War federal government fall short in its responsibility to the freed slaves?

The Civil Rights Bill

The Civil Rights Bill of 1866 was a measure which was vetoed by President Johnson, but had strong support of the Radical Republicans. "It declares who are citizens of the United States, defines their rights, prescribes penalties for violating them, and provides the means of redress." (*Harper's Weekly* editorial, April 14, 1866)

Summary:
Summarize this passage in your own words.

Harper's Weekly editorial

The Civil Rights bill declares that all persons born in the United States, and not subject to any foreign power, excluding Indians not taxed, are citizens of the United States, and that such citizens, of every race and color, "shall have the same right in every State and Territory to make and enforce contracts, to sue, to be sued, be parties, and give evidence, to inherit, purchase, lease, sell, hold and convey real and personal property, and to be entitled to full and equal benefit of all laws and proceedings for the security of person and property as is enjoyed by white citizens, and shall be subject to like punishments, pains and penalties, and to none other, any law, statute, ordinance, regulation, or custom to the contrary notwithstanding."

The bill then defines the method of protecting these rights, the details of which, if imperfect, can readily be corrected. It leaves the adjustment of political privilege to the States. It does not say that a citizen shall be a voter: it says only that he shall have the equal rights of a man.

This law, which was passed by an imposing vote in both Houses, 33 to 15 in the Senate, and 122 to 41 in the House, unquestionably expresses the profound determination of the people of the United States. They conferred freedom, and they have now defined what they

"Outside of the Galleries of the House of Representatives During the Passing of the Civil Rights Bill." (*Harper's Weekly*, April 28, 1866.)

mean by freedom. If a man can not own property and exercise every right that springs from its possession he is not free. This truth is fully recognized by Alexander H. Stephens, at whose instance, and against the wishes of many leaders, the Georgia Legislature has passed a bill legalizing equal civil rights to the freedmen. What Georgia has wisely done for itself the United States have done for the whole country. In doing it Congress has secured one of the most legitimate results of the war, and has laid the corner-stone of enduring peace and Union.

Source: *Harper's Weekly*, April 21, 1866, p. 243.

Consider this:
Study the article and graphic from *Harper's Weekly* presented here. How would the passing of the Civil Rights Bill have been presented to the nation today? What advances have we made in communications in the past 140 years? Have we lost anything with the advent of radio, TV, and the internet? Explain.

The Reconstruction Act

Congressional Reconstruction Policy

The Joint Committee drafted a plan to readmit the ex-Confederate States. At first, their plan required that the Southern states ratify the Fourteenth Amendment to gain re-admittance. However, this policy proved unsuccessful. After nearly a year, only Tennessee had ratified the Amendment. The Radical Republicans in Congress proposed another plan. Over a Presidential veto, Congress passed the Reconstruction Act, which divided the South into military districts. This plan required that the Southern states write new constitutions and form new govenments, before they could be considered for re-admission. By 1870, all the Southern states had been readmitted. Federal troops remained in the South until 1877, to protect the civil rights of Negroes.

In 1867, Frances Butler Leigh wrote a letter in which she stated her views on the Congressional Reconstruction Policy.

Consider this:
What was Leigh's main objection to the Reconstruction Act?

We are, I am afraid, going to have terrible trouble by-an-by with the negroes, and I see nothing but gloomy prospects for us ahead. The unlimited power that the war has put into the hands of the present Government at Washington seems to have turned the heads of the party now in office, and they don't know where to stop. The whole South is settled and quiet, and the people too ruined and crushed to do anything against the government, even if they felt so inclined, and all are returning to their former peaceful pursuits, trying to rebuild their fortunes, and thinking of nothing else. Yet the treatment we receive from the Government becomes more and more severe every day, the last act being to divide the South into five military districts, putting each under the command of a United States General, doing away with all civil courts and law.

Source: Frances Butler Leigh, *Ten Years on a Georgia Plantation After the War*. London: R. Bentley and Son, 1883.

A Southerner's point of view

A look at Reconstruction from a white southerner's point of view is offered in this excerpt.

The worst that the people of the South anticipated was being brought back into the union with their property gone and their wounds yet smarting. The sense of defeat, together with the loss of property by force of arms, which left them almost universally impoverished, and the distribution of their social system, was no little burden for them to bear; but it was assumed bravely enough, and they went to work with energy and courage, and even with a certain high-handedness. They started in on the plantations, where by reason of the disorganization of all labor they were needed, as wagoners or ploughmen or blacksmiths. They went to the cities, and became brakemen or street-car drivers, or watchmen or porters. Or they sought employ on public works in any capacity; men who had been generals even taking places as axemen or teamsters till they could rise to be superintendents and presidents. But they had peace and hope....

The Freedmen's Bureau and its work soon had the whole South in a ferment. The distribution of rations relieved the slaves, but misled them into thinking that the government would support them, whether they worked or not....

The white race were not allowed the franchise again until they had assented to giving the black race absolute equality in all matters of civil right. This the leaders of the other side vainly imagined would perpetuate their power, and for a time it almost promised to do so.

The result of the new regime thus established in the South was such a riot of rapine and rascality as had never been known in the

(continued on next page)

Vocabulary:
ferment = an agitated (very active) state
rapine = plunder, seizure of another's property

Vocabulary:

cupidity = greed; avarice

levies = imposing taxes

pillage = take over property by violent means

suppress = subdue; crush; put an end to

writ of habeas corpus = a legal document that brings a party before a judge to release him from unlawful restraint

history of this country, and hardly ever in the history of the world.... The states were given over to pillage at the hands of former slaves, led largely by adventurers whose only aim was to gratify their vengeance of their cupidity.

....

Unable to resist openly the power of the National government that stood behind the carpet-bag governments of the states, the people of the South resorted to other means which proved for a time more or less effective. Secret societies were formed, which, under such titles as the "Ku Klux Klan," the "Knights of the White Camellia," the "White Brotherhood," etc., played a potent and, at first, it would seem, a beneficial part in restraining the excesses of the newly exalted leaders and their excited levies.

Wherever masked and ghostly riders appeared, the frightened negroes kept under cover. The idea spread with rapidity over nearly all the South, and the secret organizations, known among themselves as the "Invisible Empire," were found to be so dangerous to the continued power of the carpet-bag governments, and in places so menacing to their representatives personally, that the aid of the National government was called in to suppress them.

In a short time every power of the government was in motion, or ready to be set in motion, against them. "Ku Klux Acts" were passed; presidential proclamations were issued; the entire machinery of the United States courts was put in operation; the writ of habeas corpus was suspended in those sections where the Ku Klux were most in evidence, and Federal troops were employed....

Source: Thomas Nelson Page, "The Southern People During Reconstruction," *Atlantic Monthly*, Vol. 88, September, 1901.

The Ku Klux Klan

Ku Klux Klan members, 1868

Testimony taken at a Senate Hearing on terrorist activity

Elias Hall recounts his terrifying encounter with the Ku Klux Klan in South Carolina.

Question. State whether at any time men in disguise have come to the place where you live, and, if so, what they did and said. First, state when it was.

Answer. On the night of the 5th of last May, after I had heard a great deal of what they had done in that neighborhood, they came. I could not understand what they said, for they were talking in an outlandish and unnatural tone, which I had heard they generally used at a negro's house.... I heard them knocking around in her [my sister-in-law's] house. I was lying in my little cabin in the yard. At last I heard them have her in the yard. She was crying, and the

(continued on next page)

Consider this:
Despite the fact that the Ku Klux Klan (KKK) was violent to Elias Hall on the night they came to frighten him, they wanted him to pray for them. Do you know of any people who do bad things to others, yet still consider themselves to be good Christians? Explain.

Ku-Klux were whipping her to make her tell where I lived. I heard her say, "Yon is her house." ...Some one then hit my door. It flew open. One ran in the house, and stopping about the middle of the house, which is a small cabin, he turned around as it seemed to me as I lay there, awake, and said "Who's here?" Then I knew they would take me, and I answered, "I am here." He shouted for joy, as it seemed, "Here he is! Here he is! We have found him!" and he threw the bedclothes off of me and caught me by one arm, while another man took me by the other and they carried me into the yard between the houses, my brother's and mine, and put me on the ground beside a boy. The first thing they asked me was, "Who did that burning? Who burned our houses?" gin-houses, dwelling-houses and such. Some had been burned in the neighborhood. I told them it was not me; I could not burn houses; it was unreasonable to ask me. Then they hit me with their fists, and said I did it, I ordered it.... After they had staid in the house for a considerable time, they came back to where I lay and asked if I wasn't afraid at all. They pointed pistols at me all around my head once or twice, as if they were going to shoot me, telling me they were going to kill me, wasn't I ready to die? and willing to die" didn't I preach? ... [they] asked if I was ready to die. I told them that I was not exactly ready; that I would rather live; that I hoped they would not kill me that time.... They all had disguises on.... Then they gathered around and told me to pray for them. I tried to pray. They said "Don't you pray against Ku-Klux, but pray that God may forgive Ku-Klux. Don't pray against us. Pray that God may bless and save us."

Source: "A Report of the Joint Committee to Inquire into the Conditions of Affairs in the Late Insurrectionary States," Washington, 1872, Vol. III.

Blacks in Office

Hiram R. Revels became the first African American elected to the Senate, in 1870. He served the unexpired term of Jefferson Davis.

During Reconstruction, African Americans were elected to public office. However, public opinion was not in their favor. Many whites argued that their lack of education and skills prevented them from carrying out their political jobs effectively.

The first African American to be elected to the United States Senate was Hiram R. Revels of Mississippi. Many Senators expressed opposition to the seating of Revels. They cited the fact that Revels did not meet the constitutional requirement of being a U. S. citizen for nine years prior to becoming a Senator. According to the law, African Americans had just recently attained citizenship, a point used by critics to try to block Revels from being seated. In the following passages taken from debates in the U. S. Senate and House of Representatives, Senator Garret Davis of Kentucky and Senator James Nye of Nevada express their opposing opinions on seating a "Negro" in the United States Senate.

Summary:
This is bad for the government. This is the first time in our history that a Black man wants to take office. Did the people of Mississippi elect him? No!

Vocabulary:
morbid = gloomy, unwholesome

Senator Davis of Kentucky

Mr. President, this is certainly a morbid state of affairs. Never before in the history of this government has a colored man been elected to the Senate.... To-day for the first time one presents himself and asks admission to a seat in it. How does he get here? Did he come here by the free voices by the spontaneous choice of the free people of Mississippi? No, sir; no. The sword of a military dictator has opened the way for his easy march to the Senate of the United States....

Summary:
It seems to me that this is a great moment, long sought-after.

If we are all brothers, of whatever race, then anyone can be elected to serve in our government. Are you, Mr. Davis, afraid of competition from colored men?

Senator James Nye of Nevada replies to Davis of Kentucky

Sir, it seems to me that this is the crowning glory of a long series of measures. It seems to me that this is the day long looked for, when we put into practical effect the theory that has existed as old as man. We say that all men are brothers; whatever their color all are subject to the same law, and all are eligible to fill any place within the gift of the people.

Is the honorable Senator from Kentucky afraid to enter in the race for future glory with these colored men?...

Source: Emma Lou Thombrough, ed., *Black Reconstructionists*. Englewood Cliffs, NJ: Prentice-Hall, 1972.

Carpetbaggers and Scalawags

by Cheryl Edwards

Reconstruction governments were made up of African Americans, white southerners, and northerners. The northerners who went South to serve in the Reconstruction governments were called carpetbaggers, because they carried their belongings in large cloth bags. Most carpetbaggers were good people who wanted to help both blacks and whites. Some worked for the Freedmen's Bureau, others were businessmen who came to invest their money. Also, many ex-Union soldiers decided to stay and help rebuild the South. Many white southerners resented the carpetbaggers, primarily because they disliked northerners running their governments, and disapproved of the carpetbaggers' acceptance of African Americans as their equals.

Scalawags were southern natives who worked with African Americans and white southerners for their own personal gain. Most wanted to make fast money and gain political power. They often took advantage of people and gained a reputation of being ruthless.

Horace Greeley Campaigns

In 1872, the Liberal Republicans nominated Horace Greeley, a newspaper editor, to run as their presidential candidate. Greeley ran against President Grant, a Republican. During the campaign, Grant was blamed for the failure of Reconstruction. Carpetbaggers were also blamed and were an easy target for critics. In this excerpt from a speech given by Horace Greeley in 1871, Greeley attacks carpetbaggers.

The thieving carpet-baggers are a mournful fact; they do exist there, and I have seen them. They are fellows who crawled down South in the track of our armies, generally at a very safe distance in the rear; some of them in sutler's wagons; some bearing cotton permits; some of them looking sharply to see what might turn up; and they remained there. They at once ingratiated themselves with the blacks, simple, credulous, ignorant men, very glad to welcome and to follow any whites who professed to be

(continued on next page)

Vocabulary:
credulous = gullible, believing too readily
ingratiated = got into the good graces
sutler = a camp follower who peddled provisions to soldiers

Vocabulary:

ascendancy = domination

jaundiced = jealous, prejudiced

paltry = petty, worthless

Source: Excerpted from the *Chicago Tribune,* which serialized the speech on June 14, July 18, 24, August 14, 26, 1872. From *Those Terrible Carpetbaggers*, by Richard Nelson Current, New York: Oxford University Press, 1988.

the champions of their rights. Some of them got elected Senators, others Representatives, some Sheriffs, some Judges, and so on. And there they stand, right in the public eye, stealing and plundering, many of them with both arms around negroes, and their hands in their rear pockets, seeing if they cannot pick a paltry dollar out of them....

What the Southern people see of us are these thieves, who represent the North to their jaundiced vision, and, representing it, they disgrace it. They are the greatest obstacle to the triumph and permanent ascendancy of Republican principles at the South, and as such I denounce them.

Albert Griffin, a Republican from Georgia, defends the carpetbaggers

Vocabulary:

cabal = conspiracy; group of plotters

malcontents = discontented with current conditions

Source: Excerpted from the *New York Times,* November 15, 1972; Albert Griffin, "The Infamous Carpet-bag Government," *Kansas Magazine*, September 1872. Found in *Those Terrible Carpetbaggers*, by Richard Nelson Current, New York: Oxford University Press, 1988.

The negroes are Southern people—natives, mostly—and even the so-called carpet-baggers are as much entitled to be a part of the people as are a majority of the inhabitants of this State [Kansas] to be called Kansans,...It seems strange indeed to hear recent settlers in the West quietly assume that those who have gone South since the war are not a part of the people where they reside, and have no political rights, except to pay taxes and vote for those who despise and revile them. But it is stranger still to try to realize that Horace Greeley, Theodore Tilton, and others with like record, in looking South for "the people," can now see none but ex-Rebels and their allies; that in their eyes, the colored men they have pleaded for so eloquently, and the union soldiers they have so often, so justly and so highly praised, have suddenly become nobodys merely because the Republican party refused to be dictated to by a cabal of malcontents respecting the renomination of President Grant.

Song about Carpetbaggers

The *Yazoo Banner,* a Democratic newspaper in Yazoo City, Mississippi, printed these verses from a song about carpetbaggers. The song mocks Charles Morgan, a Wisconsinite who came to Mississippi, and who was considered a "Yankee outcast" by the southern whites.

> Old Morgan came to the Southern land
> With a little carpet-bag in his hand.
> Old Morgan thought he would get bigger
> By running a saw-rnill with a nigger.

The chorus went, in part:
> If you belong to the Ku Klux Klan,
> Here's my heart and here's my hand.

Carl Schurz was a leading liberal, born in Germany, who moved from Wisconsin to Missouri. (Library of Congress)

Things to do:
Choose a topic from the Reconstruction period and draw your own cartoon. You can keep it simple by using "stick figures." Remember to use a caption, or words and numbers in the cartoon, where appropriate.

President Johnson's Impeachment Trial

Much to the dismay of Radical Republicans, Democrat Andrew Johnson vetoed many of the bills passed by the Radicals, insisting that they were unconstitutional and in violation of the rights of southern whites. As they gained strength, overriding the President's vetoes, Radicals began a movement aimed at removing him from office. In March of 1867, the passage of the Tenure of Office Act brought additional pressure on Johnson's presidency. The Act stated that a president must get the approval of the Senate before removing an official who had been approved by the Senate. When Johnson tried to remove Secretary of War Edwin Stanton, who supported the Radical Republicans, the House of Representatives voted to impeach the President—for the first time in our nation's history.

The trial which ensued in the Senate had to prove by two-thirds majority that the president was guilty of "high crimes and misdemeanors," in order for him to be removed from office. (Thirty-six of the fifty-four Senators would have to cast a vote of "guilty.")

On March 5, 1868, Chief Justice Salmon Chase swore the Senators in as jurors. They heard arguments from both sides until May 16th, when the final vote was to be taken. By this time only one vote was left to be counted, that of Kansas Senator Edmund G. Ross. Six Republican Senators had already voted for acquittal. When Ross, also a Republican, voted "not guilty," Johnson was allowed to remain in office *by a one vote margin!*

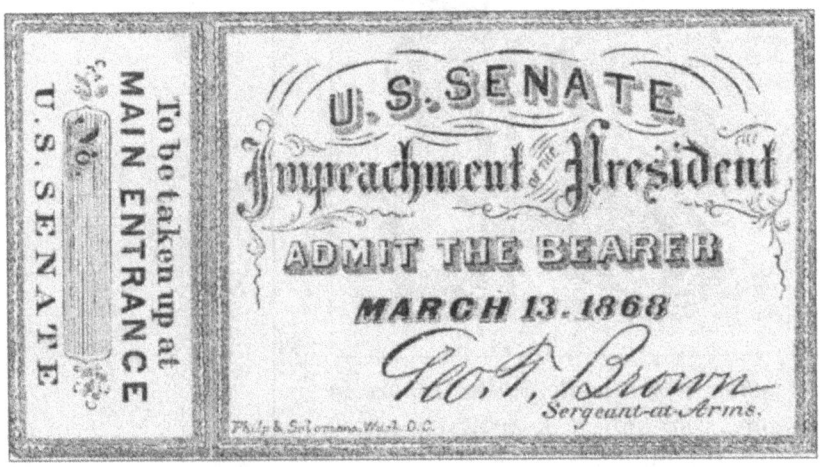

Tickets to the various sessions of the impeachment hearings were hard to obtain. Reporters and interested citizens from all over the country were anxious to watch the proceedings. Harper's Weekly *printed this facsimile of one on the tickets in its newspaper.*

George Clemenceau, a correspondent for a French newspaper who had covered the hearings, summed up the situation following the trial.

Andrew Johnson

Consider this:
Compare Johnson's impeachment trial to President Clinton's, by the use of primary source documents. You can find them on the internet and in the library.

Vocabulary:
mentor = a trusted counselor or guide
renegade = someone who deserts a party or a cause

May 29, 1868. At last the President's trial is over. The seven renegades, as the organs of the radical party call their Senators who voted for acquittal, are in the most embarrassing position imaginable. ....Very fortunately, Mr. Johnson seems much cooled down and calmed. He is satisfied with having got off with a fright and will probably not attempt any new outbreaks. It is said that he is thinking of changing his cabinet, but this is not likely. Mr. Seward is, and will continue to be, Mr. Johnson's mentor. The influence, or at least the maneuvers, of the Secretary of State played a considerable part in the President's acquittal, and one does not shut the door of one's house on a man who has just saved one's life. Besides, nothing would ever fill up the gulf that yawns between Mr. Johnson and the radicals.

The wisest course would be to try, not to understand each other, since that could not be, but at least to live in peace side by side, for the few months which they still have to spend together. Both sides must understand this simple truth.

The Black Vote
by Cheryl Edwards

In 1870, the Fifteenth Amendment became law. African American males had finally won the right to vote, but problems arose in the southern states over this law. Many felt that African Americans should not have been given the vote so soon after emancipation. Critics believed that since most African Americans were illiterate, they could not understand politics. There were also lingering tensions between ex-Confederates, who were stripped of their voting rights, and the new voters.

Myrta Lockett describes dishonest voting practices that took place in the South.

Vocabulary:
incendiary = capable of causing fire
plurality = a large number
vexation = annoyance

The Southern ballot-box was the new toy of the Ward of the Nation; the vexation of housekeepers and farmers, the despair of statesmen, patriots, and honest men generally. Elections were preceded by political meetings, often incendiary in character, which all one's servants must attend. With election day, every voting precinct became a picnic-ground, to say no worse. Negroes went to precincts overnight and camped out. Morning revealed reinforcements arriving. All sexes and ages came afoot, in carts, in wagons, as to a fair or circus....The instant polls opened they were marched up and voted.

Negroes almost always voted in companies. A leader, standing on a box, handed out tickets as they filed past. All were warned at Loyal Leagues to vote no ticket other than that given by the leader, usually a local preacher who could no more read the ballots he distributed than could the recipients.

. . . .

Negroes were carried by droves from one county to another, one State to another, and voted over and over wherever white plurality was feared. Other tricks were to change polling-places suddenly, informing the negroes and not the whites; to scratch names from registration lists and substitute others. Whites would walk miles to a registration place to find it closed; negroes, privately advised, would have registered and gone....

....

The most lasting wrong reconstruction inflicted upon the South was in the inevitable political demoralization of the white man. No one could regard the ballot-box as the voice of the people, as a sacred thing. It was a play-thing, a jack-in-the-box for the darkeys, a conjurer's trick that brought drinks, tips and picnics. It was the carpet-bagger's stepping-stone to power. The votes of a multitude were for sale....

....

According to election law, when ballots polled exceeded registration lists, a blindfolded elector would put his hand in the box and withdraw until ballots and lists tallied. Many tissue ballots could be folded into one and voted as a single ballot; a little judicious agitation after they were in the box would shake them apart.

...Democrats and Republicans had each a manager. The Republican ran his hand into the box and gave it a stir; straightway it became so full it couldn't be shut, ballots falling apart and multiplying themselves. The Republicans laughed: "I have heard of self-raising flour. These are self-raising ballots."

Source: Myrta Lockett, *Dixie After the War.* Boston: Houghton Mifflin Company, 1937.

Consider this:
Where have you read about "crooked" voting practices in the world today? Look into past president Jimmy Carter's role in keeping elections honest in other countries.

Vocabulary:
conjurer = one who practices magic
demoralization = weakened in spirit
judicious = sensible, wise

Although the new Reconstruction policies and federal laws were meant to achieve racial equality for Blacks and Whites, many were not yet ready to accept these drastic changes. The repercutions of Reconstruction were to resound well into the 20th century, with test after test of the laws to surface and be resolved and often challenged once again in the Supreme Court of the United States.

Research Activities/Things to Do

- Many whites were confused about the legal status of the freed slaves after the war. How did the Black Codes, established in several of the southern states, further complicate the issues?

- Although Blacks were being educated for the first time (with the help of the Freedmen's Bureau), their schools fell far short of those for Whites. Do you think that equal education for Blacks at that time would have made the integration process easier and swifter?

- A dangerous development in the South, after the war, was the formation of the "Invisible Empire," made up of groups like the KKK. Why do you think members of these organizations wished to remain anonymous?

- Research some of the first Blacks to be elected to public office in the South. Find out what proportion of today's elected officials are Black. How many members of Congress are of Hispanic or Asian descent?

- The Thirteenth Amendment abolished slavery, but it took the Fourteenth Amendment to make Blacks U. S. citizens. The Fifteenth Amendment gave Blacks the right to vote. Despite all of these amendments, many southerners attempted to "get around" these laws. Show documentation of this.

- Following are some thoughts expressed by freed slaves, recalling their lives and their new-found freedom. (They were interviewed in the 1930s, as part of the Federal Writers' Project.) Compare the four selections below, and comment on what parts of each you agree or disagree with.

Source: All four excerpts were taken from *We Lived in a Little Cabin in the Yard*, Belinda Hurmence, ed., John F. Blair, Winston Salem, NC, 1994

"...if slavery had lasted it would have been pretty tough. As it was some fared good, while others fared common—you know, slaves who were beat and treated bad. God is punishing some of them old suckers and their chillun right now for the way they used to treat us poor colored folks.

" I think by Negro getting educated he has profited, and this here younger generation is going to take nothing off these here poor white folks when they don't treat them right, because now this country is a free country; no slavery now."

– Susie Byrd, p. 7.

"Some of the [freed slaves] leave when they learn they can go, but us stay where us was born and bred, and live in the same fine house and do the same kind of work; but us get real money for it—a hundred dollars a year. Then us was our own boss, and could come and go like any white...."

– Henry Johnson, p. 42.

" I think these twentieth-century white folks that have principle are trying to make amends to Negroes, to make up for the meanness their foreparents done to us, so I try to forgive them all in my heart for the sake of a few good ones now."

– Levi Pollard, p. 69.

"Dixon [our master] never told us we was free, but at the end of the year he gave my father a gray mule he had ploughed for a long time and part of the crop....Folks just went wild when they got turned loose....

"I do vote. I vote a Republican ticket. I sell eggs or a little something and keep my taxes paid up. It looks like I'm the kind of folks the government would help—them that works and tries hard to have something—but seems like they don't get no help. They wouldn't help me if I was about to starve."

– Luke D. Dixon, pp. 53-4.

Before the 60's
by Ken Siegelman

In an effort more to heal the wounds
Between the North and South
Than to tell it like it was,
Real life Blacks were overlooked —
And what sly rebellious minds
Might have schemed to free themselves
Were hushed inside the silence
Of historians who thought it fruitful
To imagine docile older men with banjoes;
Children dancing in fine clothes
'round fat women who never frowned
As their fantasy of Slavery.

- Why does the poet suggest that the real-life history of Blacks in America was ignored or overlooked in the decades after the Civil War?

- What role did historians have in creating stereotypes of Blacks?

Analyzing Graphics Worksheet

Some or all of the following will help you to analyze an historic illustration. Use the worksheet to jot down notes about the piece being evaluated.

1. **What is the subject matter?**

2. **What details provide clues?**
   - ❏ scene
   - ❏ clothing
   - ❏ style of graphic
   - ❏ B&W/color
   - ❏ buildings
   - ❏ artifacts
   - ❏ written message
   - ❏ people
   - ❏ time of day
   - ❏ season

3. **Can you determine the location?   The intended audience?**

4. **What is the date? If there is no date, can you guess the period?**

5. **What is the purpose of the illustration?**
   - ❏ private use
   - ❏ art
   - ❏ recording an event
   - ❏ advertising
   - ❏ propaganda
   - ❏ Other_____

6. **Can you tell anything about the point of view of the graphic?**
   - ❏ social
   - ❏ recreational
   - ❏ political
   - ❏ sales tool
   - ❏ educational

7. **What details make this piece effective or ineffective?**

8. **What can you learn about the people who lived at this time from the illustration?**

9. **Are any symbols used in the graphic? Are they verbal or visual? Describe what each symbol represents.**

   Object   Symbolizes

The Senate as a court of impeachment for the trial of Andrew Johnson, sketched by Theodore K Davis, Harper's Weekly, April 11, 1868, pp. 232-3.

Suggested Further Reading

The books listed below are suggested readings in American literature, which tie in with *Reconstruction - Researching American History*. The selections were made based on feedback from teachers and librarians currently using them in interdisciplinary classes for students in grades 5 to 12. Of course, there are many other historical novels and nonfiction that would be appropriate to tie in with the titles in this series.

* *Amos Fortune: Free Man*, Elizabeth Yates

* *Shades of Gray*, Carolyn Reeder

* *The Autobiography of Miss Jane Pittman*, Ernest J. Gaines

* *A Cold Sassy Tree*, Olive A. Burns

* *The Unvanquished*, William Faulkner

* *Gone with the Wind*, Margaret Mitchell

* *Souls of Black Folk*, W.E.B. DuBois

* *Reconstruction: Binding the Wounds,* Cheryl Edwards, ed.

* *Those Terrible Carpetbaggers*, Richard N. Current, ed.

For information on other titles from Discovery Enterprises, Ltd., call or write to: Discovery Enterprises, Ltd., 31 Laurelwood Drive, Carlisle, MA 01741 Phone: 978-287-5401 Fax: 978-287-5402 E-mail: ushistorydocs@aol.com

www.ingramcontent.com/pod-product-compliance
Lightning Source LLC
Chambersburg PA
CBHW081022040426
42444CB00014B/3315